I0621435

the Hummingbird REVIEW

www.thehummingbirdreview.com

Volume III/number 1
2012

Ri
PUBLISHING

Published by Ri Publishing, Laguna Woods, CA, USA
www.thehummingbirdreview.com

The Hummingbird Review presents fine writing by both new writers and fully established literary figures. The review is committed to portraying the beauty and challenges of life—the full human experience—through literature and art, and promotes cross-cultural writing in all forms.

Publisher/executive editor
Charles Redner

Editor
Thea Iberall

Associate Editors
Elia Esparza
Said Leghlid

Permissions:

"When the Leather is a Whip," from *Imagine the Angels of Bread*,
Martín Espada, W.W. Norton (1996)
"George Foreman: Eye of the Storm," Adam Rodman
by permission of the author
"The Evolutionary Record," from *The Sanctuary of Artemis*,
Thea Iberall, Tebot Bach (2011)

Cover painting by Judith DiGirolamo Redner, www.jdrFineArt.com
Cover designs by Terry Houseworth, www.houseworthdesign.com

© 2012 Charles Redner

ISBN: 978-0-9855583-0-7

WHEN THE LEATHER IS A WHIP

Martín Espada

At night,
with my wife
sitting on the bed,
I turn from her
to unbuckle
my belt
so she won't see
her father
unbuckling
his belt

CONTENTS

www.thehummingbirdreview.com
Volume III/number 1
2012

CONTEXTUAL POETRY

SCREENPLAY

PROSE

PUBLISHER'S STATEMENT

Imbai nheketerwa kurumbidza mazwi

Sing Praise for the Words!

A light breeze floated across Zimbabwe, picked up speed in Botswana, darted north over Egypt, sailed west to Morocco, and then blew across the Atlantic. A zephyr carried voices of Africa to our ears and into our hearts. Two African poets sharing their verses; an American screenwriter conveying his behind-the-scenes treatment, Hollywood-style, of Ali and Foreman's "Rumble in the Jungle;" and a woman studying elephants, like Goodall studied chimpanzees, cram this issue with unique views as diverse as the continent itself. Wonder along with us as Brian Wilkes ponders tribal customs of the Cherokee Nation that match those of Berbers (Imazighen) living in the Atlas Mountains. Be sure to read Moroccan-born Said Leghlid's talk with Professor Noam Chomsky who looks beyond the obvious to help us understand the causes and possible aftermath of the Arab Spring.

Called the "Blue Marble" when viewed from space, our swirling, spinning world is most often shown with the Americas centered and thought you'd like to see Earth from another vantage, one where it all began for the human race—Africa. For our cover art, we thank oil painter Judith DiGirolamo Redner for her unique "Earth from on High" interpretations.

The poets have stormed the castle once again; in addition to the verses from Africa we discovered Indian poet, Farzana Versey and Laguna Beach actor, performance poet, John Gardiner plus a dozen poets who spear us with their wisdom, wit, pathos and humor. Perhaps even one or two poems from my files have slipped by the editors as well. Hopefully "World Peace Interrupted" made the cut. It was inspired by and is dedicated to my personal poet-sensei, Taylor Mali to whom I emailed the poem appropriately while he was teaching in India. For editor Thea Iberall we create a new section, Contextual Poetry, the likes of which we haven't seen since Charles Darwin's grandfather. Check it out.

Gratitude to Zimbabwe poet, Batsirai Chigama for the Shona translation of "Sing praise for the words," and be sure to read "Homelands," her poetic-perspective on life in Africa.

Shona is a Bantu language, native to the Shona people of Zimbabwe and southern Zambia; the term is also used to identify peoples who speak one of the Shona language dialects.

As always, I am amazed with the excellence of the words sent our way to fill out each issue. Be amazed with me and enjoy. I sincerely hope you find our efforts worth the time and treasure expended.

Charles Redner
Publisher
Laguna Woods, CA

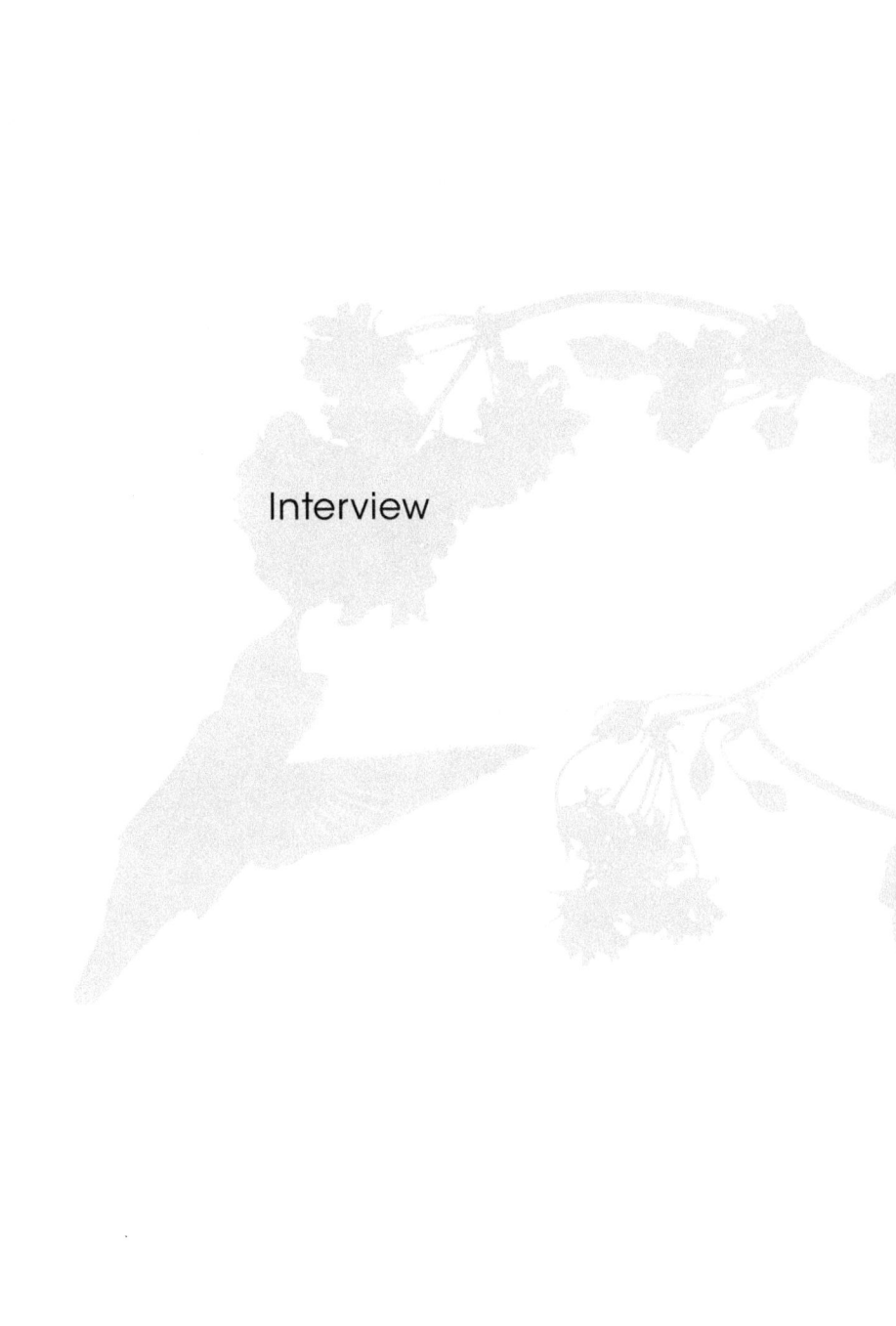

Interview

A Conversation with Professor Noam Chomsky

Said Leghlid

Moroccan-born, Hummingbird Review editor Said Leghlid, with a keen personal interest in the Arab Spring and current Middle East events, has interviewed Professor Noam Chomsky many times for WorldStreams Radio. Here Said covers the insurrection in Syria, Arab Spring, and other political issues with emphasis on human rights and Chomsky's thoughts on U.S. policy in the region.

THE HUMMINGBIRD REVIEW: *Professor Chomsky, when you look at places such as Syria and Iran, how does one justify the principles of nonintervention? Or if one intervenes might the intervener cause conditions to become worse instead of better?*

NOAM CHOMSKY: I don't think there is any formula that one can apply to such cases. One has to evaluate each case in terms of its circumstances, in terms of the likely consequences of various actions. Others might, for example, be cases where we strongly support resistances to aggression and atrocities but recognize that any effort to intervene may make the situation even worse. Those are simply complex calculations that have to be carried out in each particular case.

THR: *Regarding China and Russia, do you think they don't vote for sanctions because they are looking at the situation in Syria as getting worse?*

NC: I'm sure that they are pursuing their own state interests very much as other states do. I don't regard it as at all admirable, but I presume they are, first of all, reacting to the way in which they were basically deceived, in the case of the Libya intervention, and they were deceived. I mean, the three western imperial powers intervened under the rubric of a UN Security Council resolution which gave them essentially no authority to do what they did thinking that it was a call for a cease fire, protection of civilians, and no-fly zone that had no authorization for the direct participation as the Air Force of a rebel army leading ultimately to quite serious humanitarian catastrophes that most of the world wanted to at least try to avoid by diplomacy and negotiations. China and Russia were assured this [bombing Gaddafi forces] wouldn't happen and of course it happened right away. That's part of the reason other aspects are—in the case of Russia is its close connection with Syria. Syria provides it with a Mediterranean naval base; it's a close trading partner. Russia provides much of the arms and military aid and so on.

In the case of China, China has a quite ecumenical foreign policy. They are supporting just about everyone in their own ways. For example, they have commercial relations with Syria. They are also right at this moment, in fact, entering into fairly close relations with Israel, Syria's major enemy, on projects of development of rail connections between the Mediterranean and the Red Sea. The Mediterranean region off-shore Israel has natural gas resources that China would like. It can get them through a Red Sea connection so they are doing all these things at the same time. Now their main policy is general nonintervention and expansion of commercial and cultural relations. One can think to judge this as one likes but those are the basic policies. As far as the West is concerned, they may also recognize something which we know to be the case, whatever the intended purpose of sanctions may be, they tend generally to seriously harm the civilian population often without influencing, without affecting the ruling elite.

THR: Professor Chomsky, let's speak about Iran and its nuclear capabilities. When we look at the failure of the East and West in stopping nuclear arms and having a nuclear free world, can one even think in practical terms of a non-nuclear Iran, Israel and the rest of the Middle East? Most Iranians feel it's their right to have nuclear power for peaceful means. Secondly, the mainstream media is not mentioning the dangers from bunker buster bombs that would have to [be used] on Iran and the possible radiation leaks from bombed facilities. I have not seen this anywhere.

NC: Many of the consequences have been mentioned. I have written about them. So have others. With regard to Iran's right to develop nuclear power, it should be recognized that this overwhelming support for that in the world—the nonaligned countries, as most of the world; have been vigorously endorsing that right for years. In fact, up 'til about two years ago when the huge propaganda offensive in the U.S. began, a large majority of Americans supported it, and technically, theoretically at least, so did the U.S. and Europe.

As for ending the threat of nuclear weapons in the Middle East, that's a very important direction to pursue and most of the world is committed to a way of doing it. There is a feasible way to precede, namely, a move towards establishing a nuclear weapons free zone in the Middle East. That has the overwhelming support of the people of the region, the states of the region with the exception of Israel. The support for that internationally is so strong that at the last periodic meeting of the nonproliferation treaties almost two years ago, support was so strong that the Obama administration also had to approve of it in words at least, although they added several conditions. Hillary Clinton said at one of the meetings it's a fine idea but not now. A second condition was that Israel must be excluded from the jurisdiction of the International Atomic Energy Agency. And another condition was that no decision that's taken may require other states – meaning the United States—to provide information about the nature and the development of Israel's nuclear capacities.

Also, the Obama administration accepted Israel's condition that nothing of this sort can take place until there is a comprehensive peace settlement. Well, that can be delayed indefinitely. So yes, there is a way to proceed and there is overwhelming support for it, but it won't happen unless the major power in the world, the United States and its European allies, are willing to go along with it.

I should add something that's very rarely discussed. The United States and Britain have a unique commitment to this outcome, a very significant commitment to it. When the U.S. and Britain invaded Iraq, they did try to construct a thin legal pretext for it. The pretext was that Iraq was in violation of a UN Council resolution, Resolution 687 from 1991 which called upon Saddam Hussein to end his programs of development of weapons of mass destruction. And as you recall, for George Bush and Tony Blair and the rest of them, what they called the single question was whether Saddam had agreed to do this.

Well, we know the fate of that single question. But the point is that the U.S. and Britain did appeal to that resolution. That was the core of their legal argument. If you read that resolution, Article 14, it commits the signers to dedicate themselves to creating a nuclear weapons free zone in the Middle East. So above all others, the US and Britain have a commitment to this. Of course, they are not living up to it, but they have the commitment and that would be the reasonable way to proceed.

THR: *Obama may not be able to commit troops to fight a war with Iran. How likely it is that Israel will attack Iran and if Israel did attack, what would be the fallout in places such as Lebanon and Palestine?*

NC: Well, quite apart from the election, the U.S. is in no position to deploy armed forces troops on the ground in the Middle East or for that matter almost anywhere else. It doesn't have the capacity to do so. So, Israel is trying very hard right now to induce the United States to attack Iran. They don't want to do it themselves. They would rather have the United States do it of course. And the United States so far is apparently refusing in trying to prevent an attack. We don't know how that will proceed. If there were an attack, it would be from a distance.

It would be bombing missiles and so on. So [it is] very unlikely that either Israel or the U.S. would try to deploy troops. The consequences for Iran would very likely be horrendous. It's what happens when a country is under attack. What goes on after that, it's unpredictable. Iran might retaliate. I wouldn't be surprised if they tried. Of course, they are not going to bomb the United States. Conceivably they could bomb Israel. They have missiles that can reach Israel.

They have threatened and they might try to close the Straits of Hormuz. No one knows if they have the capability to do so. If they did, it would of course be a huge spike in the price of oil with a tottering international economy we could figure out what that would be, and they might also make moves to undermine the U.S. occupation of Afghanistan in which they have been mostly cooperating up until now, and they might move to expand their quite considerable interest in Iraq and they might also undertake efforts at terror and sabotage of the kind that the U.S. and Israel have in fact been carrying out.

A U.S. official recently reported that the assassinations of Iranian nuclear scientists were being carried out by groups that the United States designates as terrorist groups, Iranian terrorist groups that are controlled by the Israeli intelligent services by Mossad. Once a military conflict is started, you never know where it's going to go. For example, take the [Persian] Gulf where a lot of the world's oil flows. The U.S. has a huge naval presence there in aircraft carrier and enormous military presence. It's possible that some of the small Iranian speed boats under the control of the revolutionary guard might try to damage an American aircraft carrier in retaliation. If that happened, the U.S. might go berserk and start a major attack against Iran – from a distance of course.

Or there might be something like the case of the USS *Vincennes* in 1988. It's sort of forgotten in the West. I'm not sure it's forgotten in Iran. In 1988, as part of its support for Saddam Hussein in his invasion of Iraq, the U.S. was protecting ships in the Gulf to block, to bar, to undermine the Iranian blockade effort. And in those actions, a U.S. naval vessel shot down an Iranian airliner which was in commercial airspace –no question where it was –killing U.S. citizens and killing almost 300 civilians. The *Vincennes* was then returned to the United States where the crew and the captain were given a heroes' welcome. The captain and the flight officer responsible for the shooting received metals of honor and exuberant praise from the president and so on. I'm sure the Iranians haven't forgotten that.

THR: *Absolutely. Going from Iran to Syria again, how much of a balance of power would be lost as a result of that in the region? We know that Bashar—sooner or later he will be out of power. It's just a matter of time. Where would that leave Iran?*

NC: If he were removed from power or eliminated in some fashion, it would certainly weaken Iran's influence in the region. One major result of the U.S. British invasion of Iraq was to sharply increase sectarian conflicts, Shi'ite vs. Sunni conflicts. They have been there. They have been simmering for a long time, occasionally breaking out, but they were sharply increased by the invasion.

For example, they had not been very serious inside Iraq. After the invasion, they became horrendous, and it has spread throughout the region. There is now, in fact, a growing and very clear conflict between the core Sunni dictatorships of Saudi Arabia, the Gulf Emirates, and Jordan on one side and what they've called the Shi'ite crescent. The Shi'ite crescent is based in Iran. It's now extended into Iraq. Iran was the major victor of the U.S. invasion of Iraq. It includes eastern Saudi Arabia which is mostly Shi'ite and where most Saudi oil happens to be, and it includes Bahrain. That's the reason for the crushing of the democratic uprising in Bahrain. Yesterday was the one year anniversary of it – barely mentioned in the West, a brutal repression, largely motivated by concern that the Shi'ite majority in Bahrain might achieve some democratic rights and that might extend to eastern Saudi Arabia and threaten the major supplies of energy and might move towards some form of – this is very serious.

THR: *What about some of the turmoil at least symbolically taking place in the U.S. with Occupy Wall Street? What do you make of this movement and what is the likelihood that it will have a historical impact in the long-term maybe to the point of creating a third party in the United States?*

NC: I'm inclined to say maybe it will create a second party. Today's Democrats are what used to be called moderate Republicans. The Republicans have gone so far to the right that they are hardly a traditional political party any more. They are dedicated to service for the tiny sector of the super-rich and the corporate sector. That's why they have been compelled to try to mobilize sectors of the population that have always been there but they've usually been ignored. That's why you see the farcical character of the Republican debates. The Democrats are not that far behind. They are following the same line.

As far as Occupy Wall Street is concerned, it's already had quite a significant impact. I mean, it's changed the national discourse in many ways. So now there is quite open discussion of issues that were of course always there but kind of in the margins. The enormous inequality that's developed over the past 30 years, the huge growth in the power of financial institutions –which is probably harmful to the economy –certainly has changed the sociopolitical landscape enormously. There has been a sort of vicious cycle set in motion in the late 70's accelerated by Reagan, later Bush, the two Bushes. Something similar [happened] in England with Thatcher and comparable developments in a less dramatic extent on the Continent and the same in the rest of the world. This is all part of the general neoliberal onslaught. It hit hardest in Latin America and not surprisingly, Latin America was the first region where there was a sharp resistance to it.

The last ten years Latin America has pretty much freed itself from Western control, mostly U.S. control. It's a major change in world affairs and an uprising largely against the neoliberal attacks on freedom, democracy and minimal human rights.

In the North African countries, Tunisia and Egypt, the popular uprisings were also to a large extent addressing the extremely harmful consequences of the neoliberal principles that were imposed by the dictatorships jointly with the international financial institutions and the major western power which had their usual effect –very harsh consequences for the majority of the population, enriching a very small sector with lots of corruption and great praise from the World Bank and IMF. Almost up to the days of the uprising –and it's happening in the West too, not only in the United States but in Europe with the *Indignatos* and Spain, the strikes all over Europe, the uprising in Greece and so on.

As far as the Occupy Wall Street is concerned, whether it can expand its influence and lead to the kinds of historic consequences that you're referring to, well, we don't know. You can never predict those things. It's now at a kind of turning point and the movement has to reassess their strategies to consider how they will try to reach out into broader communities and engage larger sectors of the public in the kinds of struggles that they have been spearheading. How that will play out in the next few months one never knows. We will see.

Noam Chomsky is an American linguist, philosopher, cognitive scientist, political activist, author, and lecturer. He is an Institute Professor and Professor Emeritus of Linguistics at the Massachusetts Institute of Technology. Chomsky is well known in the academic and scientific community as one of the fathers of modern linguistics.

He is the most cited living author and a well-known political dissident. He was named the world's leading intellectual by Global Intellectuals in 2005. Since the 1960s, he has become known more widely as a political dissident, an anarchist, and a libertarian socialist intellectual.

Noam Chomsky has been one of the most fearless critics of US foreign policies and has worked long and hard to raise consciousness about the unnecessary use of power and human rights violations.

Essay

The Berber Stone and the Cherokee Enigma

Brian Wilkes

My reconnection with the Berber lands of North Africa begins in the Andean provincial capital of Huaraz, Peru. I had been invited there in 1998 to help establish a medicinal plant grower's fair-market co-op. Our host, Sergio, had introduced me to a small, compact man who turned out to be Don Enrique Sanes, a traditional Quechua elder and healer. We went to bed early, planning an early morning departure into more remote areas.

After a few hours of sleep, I was awakened by Don Enrique, who was speaking in a rapid, agitated manner. He tried to slow down so I could understand, but the only words I could make out were "amarillo intenso"... intense yellow. As is the global custom of locals dealing with non-fluent foreigners, he spoke more-loudly-and-slowly for me. Still nothing.

Accepting the futility of teaching me instant Spanish, he left, and returned with Sergio, who was already awake and dressed.

"He says a spirit came to awaken him to give him a vision," Sergio translated. "He doesn't know this spirit, but it's your teacher." With that, Enrique interjected "tu maestro," your teacher.

This visiting spirit had shown Enrique an object with an unknown design. Enrique tried to draw it in the air with gestures, then got a pen and notepad. It was a rectangular, slightly trapezoidal figure, with a number of broad lines and line fragments crossing it at various angles. As Enrique drew it, it vaguely resembled a mask.

"This is a yellow cloth with dark markings, maybe black. The spirit says this is very significant to you. Is it a Cherokee emblem, perhaps?"

Not one that I had ever seen, I answered. Enrique was confounded. The spirit had been very clear, this was something very important and significant to me.

"You will understand this soon," he insisted.

While researching a news story on the web one day, I saw photos of a demonstration somewhere in the Middle East. One of the banners leapt off the screen, because it appeared to be written in Cherokee. I found as many stories on that demonstration as possible, and determined that the banner was the regional Canary Islands version of a Berber independence flag. It was black characters on intense yellow.

The Berbers are a tribal people whose lands once stretched from Mauritania on the Atlantic to Libya on the Mediterranean, and are related to the ancient Phoenicians and Carthaginians. Berbers today live scattered in many countries, but primarily in the modern nations of Morocco, Algeria, Tunisia, and Mauretania. In the first century CE, they were a seagoing people ruled by descendants of Cleopatra and Marc Antony.

I recalled old Cherokee migration legends that suggest an ancient connection with North Africa, and DNA markers in most Cherokee mixed bloods support that story. My own DNA test shows the Berber matches.

I also recalled a story told of Sequoyah, the celebrated originator of the modern Cherokee writing system. In one version, Sequoyah retold that the Cherokee once had a complete writing system, but this was gradually lost, until all that was remembered was the written representation of the name of the people, which resembles CWY. When the English encountered the ancestors in South Carolina, it was pronounce "charakee" in their lowland dialect, now extinct. The people of the mountains pronounced it "zalagee" or "jalagee," pronunciations still used today. There have been many opinions over the years of what this name means, with the two most popular being "people of the sacred fire," and "people of different speech." Cherokee is from a language family very different from its neighbors.

Almost identical characters in vowel-less Berber are what they call themselves – Amazigh, the Free People. The central character, Z, resembles a double-ended trident, a representing a tree with a root system mirroring its branches. If the roots are deep, they say, a tree can survive and grow again even if it is cut down close to the ground. That would certainly be an apt description of centuries of failed attempts by Arab rules to eradicate Amazigh culture and identity, and European attempts to do the same to the Cherokee. Berber activists sometimes abbreviate Amazigh to the central character, and then cut that in half so it resembles a W. Demonstrators frequently flash a salute with three fingers spread to form the abbreviated Z.

Some among the Cherokee believe that we were saved from a volcano and flood by sailing west on reed boats, following a seven-pointed star, and we believe we must always live in the mountains near cedar trees in case the world floods again; and we call the mountains Attala. We tell stories that our ancient homeland still exists beyond the sea.

The seven-pointed star is important in North African tradition, and is sometimes called "the star of the west." The mountains in Morocco are called Atlas, and were famous for their cedar trees. Natives of the Azores, Canaries, and other

Atlantic islands told flood evacuation stories similar to those of the Cherokee.

In the spring of 2008, a college friend, Bonnie Rankin, told me she would be traveling into the Berber communities of Morocco.

In my dealings with tribal Elders around the Americas over the past 20 years, one common custom is the exchange of stones. Each Elder ends up with a bundle of ordinary looking rocks, which maintain that Elder's connection with the people who gave the stone, and with their lands. The idea came to me that this was an opportunity to exchange stones with what might have been the ancient Cherokee homeland.

I went to Mandy Falls in Livingston County, an important site along the Trail of Tears, a few miles from the Ohio River, where I left tobacco and took a small stone. Bundling the stone in a ceremonial deerskin pouch, I wrote a letter in English and French explaining the situation and tradition, and sent both stone and letter in to Rankin, who carried the bundle on her Moroccan journey.

Through an interpreter, she explained the letter to Amina, the mistress of the Berber home in the rural Ourika Valley southeast of Marrakech, who hosted part of the trek. Amina immediately recognized the custom, brought a stone from her courtyard garden, and presented her stone in exchange, adding hugs and the French-style kiss on both cheeks for Bonnie. Amina then carefully placed the Kentucky stone in the same garden spot her gift had just vacated.

Don Enrique had been proven right. The black marking on yellow cloth had been very significant. But so was a follow-up statement.

A few days after his first cryptic revelation, I had asked about the ancient megalithic culture that had built similar structures in Peru, Yucatan, and a few other sites, as well as Cherokee similarities with Maya and pre-Incan cultures.

"Maya, Inca, Cherokee, Egyptian —all the same people," he said flatly. And then in the infuriating way of many Native American Elders, he refused to say another word on the subject.

Egyptian? Now I was really confused. How could I learn more, I asked.

"You must go to Egypt to be taught."

A few years later I moved from New Jersey to western Kentucky, to a little town on the Trail of Tears, just a few miles from the Ohio River. Early settlers had found so many mound sites, tombs, and artifacts that they called the flatter regions "Little Egypt," and gave their settlements names like Memphis, Cairo, Thebes, and Karnak.

Archaeologists soon debunked the artifacts, which included thousands of coins and tablets they thought to be crude forgeries of genuine Egyptian antiquities. But later research has shown some of the inscriptions to be Phoenician, Punic, and Numidia, languages spoken in ancient Mauretania. And the markings on the coins have proven to be not clumsy Egyptian, but the insignia of Alexander Helios – the last surviving offspring of Cleopatra and Antony.

As Don Enrique had foretold, I had indeed gone to "Egypt" to be taught.

The Kentucky stone now sits in a Berber garden in Morocco, and the Berber stone now sits in the Cherokee garden in Marion, a constant reminder of the ancient oral histories and migration sagas of the Cherokee people, as well as the lesson that connections between peoples require that someone reach out first.

We can only wonder what the Berber family thinks when they gaze at the Kentucky stone. What story will they share with generations to come?

Singing Like Yma Sumac

Cheryl Merrill

Standing on a termite mound, face-to-trunk with an elephant, I place the palm of my hand against Morula's fluttering forehead, a forehead as cool and rough as tree bark. She's burbling, a rumble that resonates like water gurgling down a hollow pipe.

She's also making sounds I can feel but not hear. Right at the top of her trunk, where her bulging nasal passage enters her skull, her skin pulses beneath my hand, vibrations that reverberate in my chest cavity, drum against my heart. Muscular groundswells of sound roll full and luxuriously out in the bush, bumping into hippos, giraffes, zebras, lions, hyenas, birds, snakes and tsetse flies.

But it is only elephants who raise their heads and listen.

Most of Morula's vocalizations are rumbles, which fall partially or entirely in the infrasonic range of 5-30 Hz., throbbing, quaking air for which we humans have no auditory perception. Such low-frequency rumbles usually have harmonics and overtones, both of which can be selectively emphasized. As in a whale song, each individual elephant has a signature sound, one like no other elephant – their voices as different from each other as our voices are different from each other.

Are you there?

And invisibly, from beyond an island of trees: *Yes, I am here.*

Speech makes us human, makes these marks on this page possible. When we speak, our vocal chords vibrate with forced, small explosions of air from our lungs. We shape words with our mouth and tongue. Expelled from a chest full of wind, words float around us like little clouds, each one a separate exhalation, creating an atmosphere of meaning, thickening language one word after another. Sounds unfold in time, in agreeable waves pulsing against our ears. When we are lost and listening to a piece of pleasurable music, time even suspends itself. Songs hang on our bones.

Standing on a termite mound, I close my eyes. The fluttering beneath my hand goes on and on and on.

I open my eyes. "MO-RU-LA," I sing.

My voice, like hers, originates in my vocal chords. But my vocal range is barely an octave, limping through the air at 220 Hz. Morula's range is tremendous, more than 10 octaves, from 5 Hz. to 9,000 Hz.

The most athletic human voice in history belonged to Yma Sumac, a Peruvian, who had a self-proclaimed range of five octaves and a recorded range of four and a half. From B below low C to A above high C, from about 123 Hz. to 1760 Hz. Sumac's high range was the same frequency as an elephant's trumpet. This is a woman who could occasionally hit a triple-trill and whose voice could sound like an upright bass.

Morula would find her vocalizations a lot more fascinating than mine are.

Like all elephants, Morula is able to produce low frequency sounds just because she is big. The larger the resonating chamber (think cello compared to violin), the lower the frequency of its sound. Morula also has long and loose vocal chords and a flexible arrangement of bones attached to her tongue and larynx. In addition to her loose voice box she also has another special structure at the back of her throat called a pharyngeal pouch, which not only affects her low-frequency tones but also holds an emergency supply of water.

Morula can produce different results from the same basic rumble by holding her mouth open or shut, by an empty or full pharyngeal pouch, by flapping her ears rapidly or slowly, by holding her head high or low, or by the position of her trunk and the speed of air moving through it. She can combine hundreds of variables to invent thousands of sounds. Imagine a vocal instrument equal parts cello, double bass, violin, tuba and trumpet, one whose entire body is an expanding and contracting resonating chamber, one that can sing with a throat full of water and triple-trill a rumble, a roar, and infrasound, all in one 3-second call.

Yma Sumac would be horribly jealous.

Straight-armed, I lean against Morula's forehead. A soothing mantle of high-pitched insect noise drapes over my shoulders.

The fluttering beneath my hand has unexpected results. A soft dry scrape makes me look around. It's Thembi's ears whisking against her shoulders. She's standing behind me, on the opposite side of the termite mound.

Glancing from one large forehead to another, from one set of eyes and back, I have a feeling Morula and Thembi are waiting for me to do something.

Maybe something as simple as rumbling in return.

Poetry

Homelands

Batsirai E. Chigama

Here is a starving child
There is a mad dog;
Feed her, bomb him …
Information about Africa reaches us
through a series of filters—
CNN,
BBC,
reducing the vast continent
To a cluster of emotive slogans
Succeeding in denying Africa,
the rest of the world,
with truth, complexity, context.

Our war was never
between the Hutus & Tutsis
We fight against
a hegemony of cartographers
Cutting borders
drawing MAPS
charting the chasms of African souls;
Against mythic figure of the foreign correspondent
Who comes here sends bad news
Too much reality for them overseas
For us too landlocked within our nations
Shocked at things he purports we do.

It is time to switch channels
Switch off accounts of horrific,
Metamorphosed realities of unknown facts,
Switch off the over-zealous journo-fantasist
Rummaging in the dustbins of Rwanda
Dead bodies litter in the minds of the young
Strewn across blooded pavements
With no one to claim them
Is this what the African life has become;
A daily escape from death, until the day we don't?
Escape?

Africa is not safe they say
Her soul is brutalized by "landmines"
Dongas gaping shamelessly
where diamonds lay; where did the diamonds go?
You may ask
Her children kneel in falling crevices
Groping for a little chuff June to May
Her vast plains are watered by sweat
Yet within all her dissected fertile being
Her children reduced to "eating rats"
Find within their hungry stomachs
Energy to dance, to laugh
Listen to the morning bird songs
And wake up to a new melody each day.

At the bira the children
Lose themselves in the throb of the jembe
Wantonly seducing life
to wrap her arms around them

Exorcising the night of her ills
This is what Africa is
Rhythm

(adapted from Salman Rushdie's essay "Homelands")

Taureg Indigo

T J Dema

I am she who wears colour on skin
Adorning flesh with desert shades of indigo
My stories tell themselves below eyes
Above buttered cheeks
I have no need for a metal sky
A casket carved of bone, mortared in blood
I am a million constellations moulded of mud
The colour of a waking sky
Purple blue memories, sand storm covered secrets
Between my lover the desert
and I

First published in Hair Power - Skin Revolution
edited by Nicole Moore - 2010

What Separates Us

Charles Redner

What separates us are
oceans and rivers for a start
mountains and fences us part.

Wavy lines on maps countries defined
where histories create past enemies of mind.

Politics offer different points of view
which fashions may not agree with you.

What separates us are
race, religion and regulations a bevy
cultural and social mores weigh heavy.

Languages generate a huge divide amongst nations
confusing simple wants for hurtful condemnations.

Sexual orientation provides a reference
but might take much to abide by another's personal
    preference.

Earthlings know that all of us must make do
upon our diminutive spinning rondure of aqua hue
wandering amid a black void so vast and great
that it must be measured by time not a tape.

For Taylor Mali in the land of Gandhi

World Peace Interrupted

Charles Redner

Imagine a poem that pursues world peace.
    RING. RING.
Thanksgiving dinner sans arguments.
A school playground without a scuffle.
Civility returns to the U.S. Congress.

Imagine a poem that elevates world peace.
    RING. RING.
Rappers remove F-bombs from their lyrics.
Folsom Prison skinheads play music on the bars.
Mississippi clansmen burn hand-me-down sheets.

Imagine a poem that promotes world peace.
Machetes melted for dinner plates in Uganda.
Fights in Thailand are over *Pad Thai* or *Woonsen*.
Tanks backup in North Korea.

Imagine a poem that advances world peace.
    RING. RING.
Cartel guns in Mexico go silent.
Harmony settles over Palestine.
War no more in Afghanistan.

Imagine a poem that encourages world peace.

Hummingbird Review

The spirit of Gandhi spreads throughout Pakistan.
Bomb-makers in Karachi bake honey cakes instead.
Al Qaeda begs forgiveness before disbanding.
I'm writing a poem to establish world peace.
    RING. RING. RING. RING.
"Hello."
        "Lennon would have turned seventy today. Imagine."
"I already have."

October 9, 2010

Hotel Room

Farzana Versey

familiar scent of strangers
leftover fingerprints
on mirrors
reflecting lost caresses
in deep wrinkles
on mattresses
burdened with guilt
tables laden with fruit
like still-life painting
soft pillows heavy
with dried tears
crumbs hidden in carpet knots
toes scrounge for bits
of buttered toast
towels remind of other bodies
wrapping wetness
from the open window
a bird flies
with clipped wings

for Anna Akhmatova

The Cats Of Leningrad

John Gardiner

January 27, 1944

Pyotr Markov had survived on a few grams of bread, more sawdust than flour. He made soup from rotting mutton, joiner's glue, leather belts, and calf skin, the stench of which he never forgot. He put pine twigs in hot water and called it tea. He chewed on raw soil near Badayevsky, where fires after German bombings had melted sugar from beet crops into the earth. He pushed aside bobbing heads floating in the Neva River when he went for water. He read Pushkin's poems to the children to distract them from hunger, and the theatres remained open even as his world seemed ending.

May 9, 2006

Walking with thousands of Russians through Saint Petersburg (no longer Leningrad), in commemoration of Victory Day and the end of the 900 day siege and over a million lives lost, I watch Markov quietly celebrating in his tattered war uniform, drinking vodka, eating brown bread and pickles, face weary and peaceful, wrinkles dug like trenches across his forehead. I ask my guide about all the statues of cats tucked away throughout the city, and she tells me: *It is our way of honoring them, thanking them for their sacrifice; they were the last of the food before we had to eat our own dead. Troy fell. Rome fell. Leningrad did not fall.*

The Cloud

Aleksandr Pushkin

1835

The last one of clouds of scattered a tempest,
Just single you're flying in azure, the prettiest,
Just single you're bringing the sorrowful shade,
Just single you're saddening day that is glad.

In nearest past, you were storming skies, mighty,
And were quite enwind by the powerful lightning,
And you were the womb for divine thunders birth,
And quenching with rain the insatiable earth.

Enough, now vanish! Your time is not endless -
The earth is refreshed and away gone the tempest;
And now the wind, fondling leaves of the trees,
With pleasure is driving you out the sky bliss.

Translated by Yevgeny Bonver, July 12, 2004

Kano to Cairo

by John Gardiner

The Sahara desert rises from below
like Dante's vision of Inferno, the plane
shakes like an elevator with a faulty shaft.
Prayer beads rattle, the engine coughs,
and out of nowhere, staring up in horror,
nomadic specters from the pock-marked sand
struggle with sacks of colored glass,
perhaps a Berber tribe with Goulamine beads
too far east of Morocco.

I can see the whites of their date-colored eyes.
They are a ghost battalion made of roots and scrub.
They are too close.

United Arab Airlines, Flight 107, is going down.
I will die in a dune—my bones will blow away,
scraps of calcium for hungry mice.
The Muslims are whispering to Allah
and juggling beads as if they were white hot.
We're going to crash and it is my fault.
They stare at me—the hideous, hairy hippie
from the West, day-glow dashiki, purple pantaloons,
green slippers with toes curling up like mutant weeds.
I look like one of Ali Baba's thieves.

When we finally land, authorities impound my passport,
seal me off in a small room and stare—
not in fear or anger—they just want to know
why I was in Ouagadougou and Bobo-Dioulasso,
Burkina Faso and Mopti, Mali.

and what I am doing in Cairo
with a weather-beaten, expired ticket to Frankfurt
and five dollars to my name.

Estate Sale

May K. Cobb

Sixty years of life
Perched on wobbly card tables
Boxed up for strangers

Transplanting

May K. Cobb

abandoned homestead
patch of lonely paper whites
rescued by shovel

Plum Tree Haiku

John Rouleau

Spring wraps the plum tree
in a pink kimono of
delicate blossoms

rainsound

John Rouleau

the sound of rain
sneaks up on me
unexpectedly
in a drought year

My Chicana Consciousness

Jackie Lopez

I hang out with Witches, Buddhists, Nudists,
and Warlocks with entrepreneurial skills.
Why, I have Chicana Consciousness,
and I know that your office will not recommend such
    indecent behavior,
unless one speaks in code to the woman
at the front desk asking for one's resume.
La vida is Carnaval,
so she just may be the power behind her glass ceiling.
Give her an apple.
You just might get the job.
Remember not to tell her you live alone in the forest.

I went home after the interview and spoke with Zeus.
And while I was dancing he speared a stake of everlasting-
    faith
in my heart.
So, now I come to you bleeding and faithful
saying:
"Good things have come about.
Do not pay attention to the wizard behind the curtain.
He is just an orator. And this blood on my apron comes
    from courage."

I'm such a curandera.
I'm about to heal myself with a kiss.
I am just so loyal and faithful to the wild woman with heart.
I know how she dances and what she looks like.
She looks like me,
and she cackles coquettishly to the unborn Masters of the
    Universe.

And how did it all begin, and what was had?
It started when I was seven years old, and the young man said,
"Take a belt to that tamed one who speaks with Barbies."
I was not inducted to the mysteries of dance until I was 3,
so I had a lot to learn.

After much reading in the closets
and much washing under faucets,
it dawned on me that there seemed to be a misconception
of how to live in the Universe Complete.
So at age 15, I prayed for wisdom and cleanliness.
At age 30, Zeus noticed me lingering
on the streets of exploitation and decided to give me
a scholarship into his arms.
I have never been the same since then.

Literary Legacy

John Perry

I thought
    they were merely words:
        rivulets of ink
    dutifully following lines on a page.
Then I heard her reading
    voice like gentle rain
        collected from the contours
            of her soul.
Thoughts rippling over
    rhythms and rhymes
Sentences plunging
    into pools of proverbs.
Eddies of irresistible ideas
    rushing toward
        revelations of love and life.
I found myself
    floating through meadows of metaphors
        fiery with daffodils and dialogue
            fragrant with pine-scent and parables.
    adrift in currents
        carrying me to a sea
            of infinite imagery.

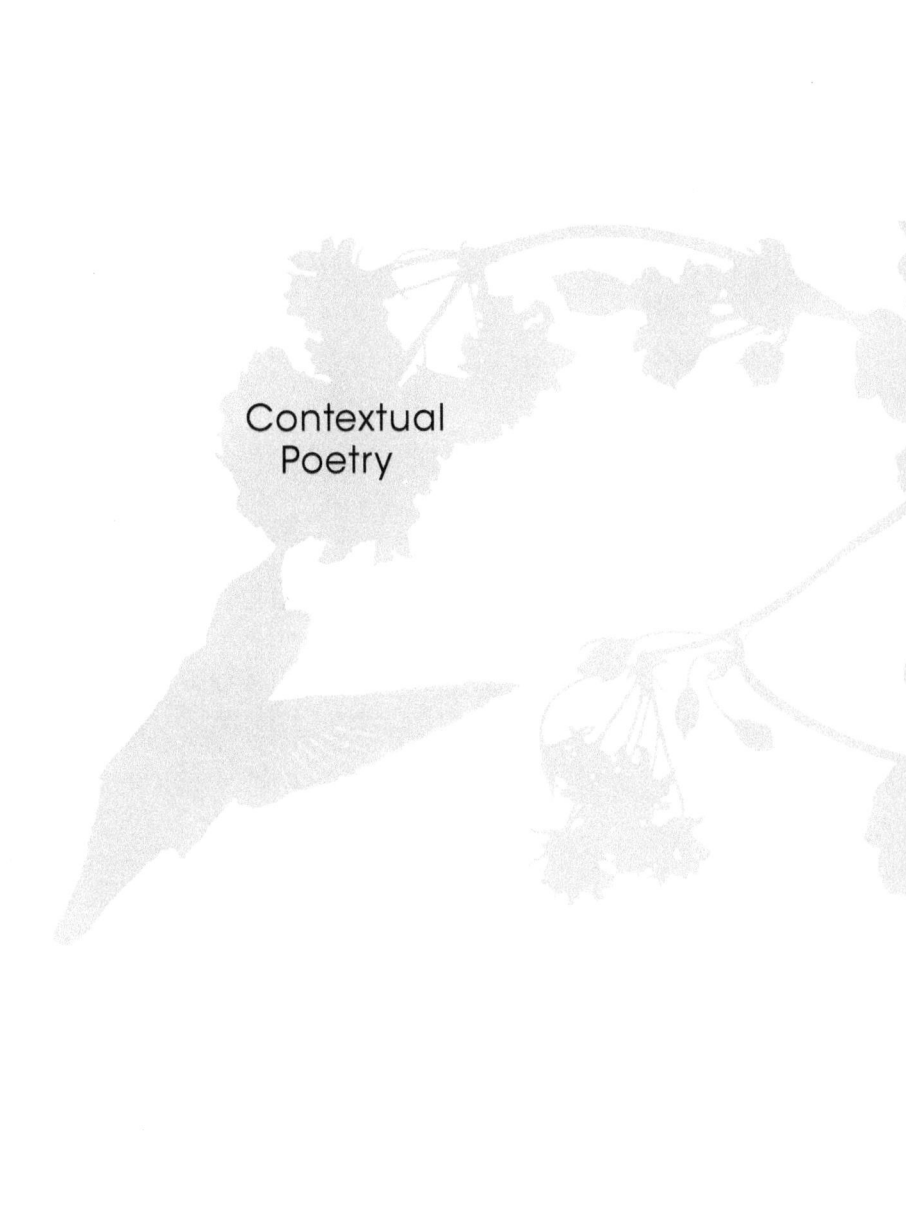

Contextual
Poetry

Contextual Poetry

As I watched Academic Honors at the University of Southern California, I was struck by contrasts. On one side was a poet exploring the roots of culture phenomena. On the other, was a scientist/engineer striving to articulate the meaning for life. The awards presenter, stumbling over complicated terms, laughingly commented, "Obviously, science is not my field." Yet, after three students played a Beethoven string trio, he mentioned how we could all appreciate music. And I thought, why is it all right that music and the arts are so accessible yet we aren't concerned that science and history are not?

We live in a world of specialists. While our body of knowledge explodes into an array of amazing discoveries, it gets parceled into finer and finer facts. If this trend continues, we will go from a people that "knows a lot about a little" to one that "knows everything about nothing." I think of myself as an educated person, having two graduate degrees in science and one in fine arts. Yet, when I read H.D.'s *Helen in Egypt*, I needed a stack of books in order to understand the poem's intense subtleties.

The boundary between the science and the arts, between history and the present is profound. As we move from an education steeped in classical knowledge to books such as *Spoonfed Stuff for Dummies*, what will happen to thousands of years of accumulated history, science, philosophy, and theology? Our libraries are bursting at the seams with digitized information, yet we increasingly live in a world of trivia: the tidbits of *Who Wants to Be a Millionaire*, fast-food restaurants, and a pill for every problem. Most onerously, so-called "facts" on the Internet proliferate and distort the truth. A publishing process with a peer-review and editorial verification cycle is being replaced by urban myths, desktop publishing, and fake testimonials. Not only are we being buried by an avalanche of data that we are unable to synthesize or comprehend, we can no longer have faith that what little we might know is true. Soon, if we are not careful, everything will be so confused that the knowledge and wisdom of the past will be lost.

We need knowledge in our lives, for ourselves as well as for future generations. But if we don't find a way to internalize it coherently, we will stumble over anything that takes too long to learn or find with our search engines. Science writers and historians try to explain the past and its discoveries. However, is there a way to go beyond explanation and achieve a true dialog? Can poets participate in this quest for wisdom and provide insights into human life against a backdrop of history?

Contextual poetry is a way to integrate the knowledge of science and history with the language of poetry. Material supporting the poem allows the writer to explore the deeper knowledge. It can be an essay, a scientific demonstration, an image. The essay should be about the same size as the poem. Beyond essay, this expands into a variety of multimedia dimensions, just as our currently static books are evolving beyond the written page into hypertext and interactive literature. The rules for writing a contextual poem are simple:

1) the context is not an explanation, notes, or an epigraph, but a jumping-off point for a dialogue of integration;

2) the context and poem together provide insights;

3) they should be able to stand alone, but resonate with each other;

4) scientific and historical references should be cited, drawn from diverse disciplines, accessible and available to an audience; and

5) experts in the pertinent fields should help evolve the context.

Contextual poetry is a poetry of boundary integration. It is a poetry of knowledge.

Dr. Thea Iberall

The Evolutionary Record

Thea Iberall

A hand can shape itself into a form
evolved for picking insects and apples

yet by the shadowed light of a fire
a woman's hand picked up a half bent reed

drove it into a mass of wet clay
marking the simple first

exchange of five of her husband's brown
goats for round tokens

leaving the other side of the slab
free to write the blood of her gender

Context

I studied the human hand for twelve years. I was fascinated by it because, in conjunction with the brain, it has built every human-made thing around us.

What is a human hand? It took about fifty-five million years for it to evolve from the mammalian paw into a prehensile masterpiece ('prehensile' means the ability to grasp). As our ancestral species was first forced into the arboreal life of the rainforest and then out onto the savannas of Africa[1] (or between arboreal and terrestrial food sources as suggested by another theory[2]), the appendage began to change: fingers became differentiated with architectural support from long tendons and uniquely shaped wrist bones. Fingertips flattened and filled with sensory receptors as small muscles became located within the hand for movements of adduction and abduction (spreading fingers out and in).[3,4] Importantly, the thumb began to shift to a position in opposition with the other fingers, slowly forming a triumvirate of thumb, index, and middle finger. What emerged was the precision grip,[5] an exquisitely crafted tool for fine manipulation. Try picking up coins, turning a small screwdriver, or opening a pill bottle—these actions all use the precision grip.

The synchronicity of what happened about 5,000 years ago still amazes me. Human society had developed the need for record keeping that would put this precision capability to use in the form of holding an implement for writing. The skill and the need coalesced into a foundation for all of written history. Interestingly, linked with the appearance of writing has been the establishment of hierarchical societies.[6] Leonard Shlain argues that literacy promotes linear and abstract thinking at the expense of more holistic and integrative views of the world. As a result, the male brain, already geared towards linear behaviors for hunting, took to (although, didn't necessarily invent) writing and was made more powerful by it. This thus formed the birth of the patriarchy. An interesting, biologically based theory.

Hands are tools that make tools. Today, with computers, will we lose the ability to write by hand? And will multimedia, image oriented languages emerge and perhaps someday create more egalitarian societies that accept all the varieties of humans?

1. Washburn. Sherwood L., Tools and Human Evolution, *Scientific American*, Sept, 1960 (Reprinted in *Human Ancestors, Readings from Scientific American*, San Francisco: W. H. Freeman and Company, 1979).

2. Kingdon, Jonathan. *Lowly Origin*, NJ: Princeton University Press, 2003.

3. Napier, John R., The Evolution of the Hand, *Scientific American*, 207(6): 56-62, 1962 (Reprinted in *Human Ancestors, Readings from Scientific American*, San Francisco: W. H. Freeman and Company, 1979).

4. Wilson, Frank R., *The Hand*, NY: Pantheon Books, 1998.

5. MacKenzie, Christine L. and Iberall, Thea, *The Grasping Hand*, NY: Elsevier-North Holland, 1994.

6. Shlain, Leonard, *The Alphabet versus the Goddess*, NY: Viking, 1998.

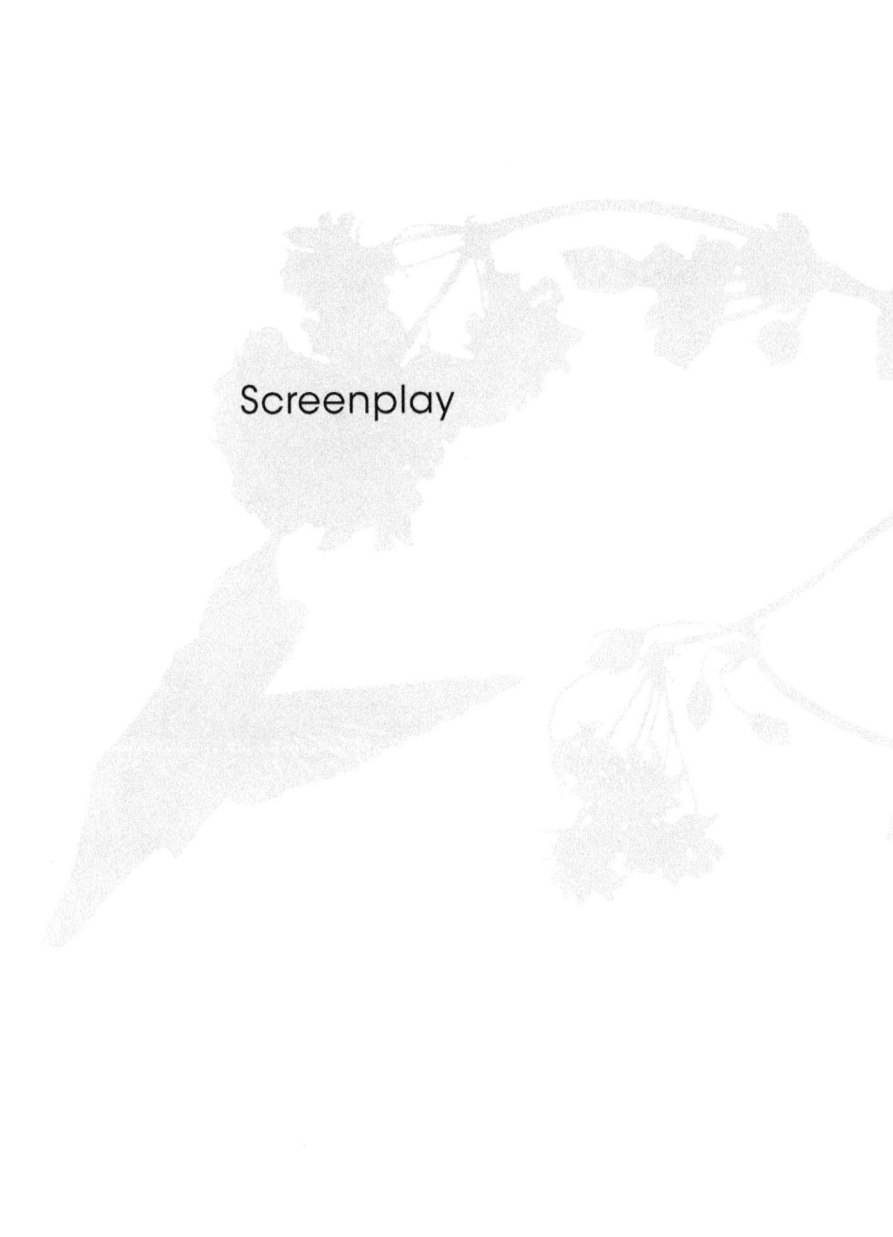

Screenplay

George Foreman: Eye of the Storm

Adam Rodman

Adam Rodman was asked to write a biographical drama about the life of George Foreman. The larger than life teddy bear selling kitchen appliances we all know and love today was a very, very different person as a younger man. Angry, filled with hate and envy that he could neither understand nor control. Foreman was headed for a collision course with disaster. Losing to Muhammad Ali in Zaire changed his life, and in the destructive wake which followed, Foreman found the internal strength to remake himself. More than anything, this is a phoenix tale, a tale of a man who would destroy himself if he didn't find a way to remake himself.

This excerpt of the screenplay depicts Foreman's downfall. It led to the most difficult period of George's life, but it also gave him the opportunity to look at himself naked, decide that he did not like the man he had become, and gradually, and with much effort, to remake himself. It is a story of incredible courage, and ultimately, of redemption.

GEORGE

You're next. I'm going to kill you! I'm going to kill you!

A camera FLASHES and the image of George in all his fury, shouting at Muhammad Ali, is caught in a photo.

FREEZE FRAME on George, his mouth contorted in rage, his gloved fist shaking at Muhammad Ali—just out of his reach.

INT. A MANSION – DAY

George is sitting at an enormous table in the kitchen, wolfing down a bowl of cereal while he peruses the sports sections of various newspapers from around the country.

INSERT - A NEWSPAPER HEADLINE

The same shot of George that we saw in the previous scene, and above it the headline: "GEORGE FOREMAN—HOW LONG BEFORE HE KILLS SOMEBODY?" GEORGE CHORTLES at the headline, enjoying his notoriety.

> GEORGE
>
> Damn straight.

The doorbell RINGS O.S. George wipes his face with his arm, goes to answer it.

INT. THE ENTRYWAY TO THE MANSION – DAY

George opens the door TO REVEAL TWO BEAUTIFUL WOMEN, dressed in scanty, sequined, red white and blue outfits.

> TWO BEAUTIFUL WOMEN
> (in unison:)
>
> Uncle Don wants you.

The women take George by the arm.

EXT. THE MANSION - DAY

The two beautiful women lead George down the steps of his mansion and toward a brand new Mercedes-Benz top of the line convertible, with a red ribbon tied on the hood: it's a gift.

George looks at the car, looks at the women.

> GEORGE
>
> You want to tell me what the hell is going on?

A phone RINGS inside the car. One of the women holds out her arm, like Vanna White turning letters. She leads him to the car, hands him the car phone.

> GEORGE
>
> Hello?

> DON KING'S VOICE
>
> George? George Foreman?

> GEORGE
>
> Who the hell is this?

> DON KING'S VOICE
>
> It's Don King here. How would you like to be rich?

> GEORGE
>
> I am rich.

> DON KING'S VOICE
>
> Rich beyond your wildest dreams.

> GEORGE
>
> I'm listening.

DON KING'S VOICE

I've got five million dollars for you to
fight Muhammad Ali. That's more money
than anyone has ever gotten for a boxing
match in history. Five million good old
U.S. of A. greenbacks, and all you got to
do is sign the papers.

One of the attractive women holds up a sheaf of papers—a
contract—which she has taken from the automobile.

GEORGE

What's with the car?

DON KING'S VOICE

It's a gift. From me to you. One brother
to another.

GEORGE

What's wrong?

DON KING'S VOICE

You insult me...

GEORGE

Just tell me what it is. Don't know one
give someone a new automobile when
they want to pay 'em five million dollars.
Not 'less there's a problem.

DON KING'S VOICE

I know you're the champ... Muhammad's
getting the same as you. That's the deal.

GEORGE

You got five million dollars for me, I ain't

gonna worry about Muhammad. You tell
Muhammad he better worry' bout his
self. He gets in the ring with me, he may
not get out still breathin'.

George hangs up the phone, looks at the two beautiful women.

GEORGE
Ladies, how'd you like to go for a drive?

EXT. THE ZAIRE AIRPORT – DAY

As a plane taxis to a stop, we SUPERIMPOSE the title:
KINSHASHA, ZAIRE, then out.

The door to the plane opens and out comes DON KING, hair in the
air, wearing a loud dashiki. MUHAMMAD ALI, also dashiki clad
is next. George EXITS the plane; he has a purebred GERMAN
SHEPHERD with him and wears the loudest dashiki of all.

As they look around we go to:

VARIOUS ANGLES - TO COVER

A THRONG of ZAIREANS has come to greet the entourage. None
of them wear dashikis. They are all dressed in Western style clothes.

George SEES this, and is immediately unhappy.

GEORGE
(to Don King)
I told you this was stupid.

Muhammad Ali is the first one down the plane steps. The CROWD
CHEERS for him, CALLS HIS NAME. Ali works the crowd,
talking with people and playing with youngsters. A Zairian official,
BULA MANDUNGU, comes forward to greet the Americans.

BULA

Mr. Foreman. Mr. King. Welcome to
Zaire. Mr. Ali. Mr. Ali.

But Ali is lost in the crowds and does not even hear. George shakes
his head, just beginning to recognize what he is going to be facing.
George's GIRLFRIEND squeezes his hand; he shakes her off.

EXT. A HIGHWAY IN ZAIRE - DAY

A long line of government limousines drives along the deserted
highway. They are flanked by military vehicles with armed
soldiers.

EXT. A GOVERNMENT COMPOUND - DAY

The limousines are parked in the courtyard. Ali and Foreman,
along with their respective ENTOURAGES, mill about as Bula
shows them their quarters. George has a large German Shepherd
with him. The ZAIREAN OFFICIALS all regard it with
mistrust. ARMED SOLDIERS patrol the fencing around the
perimeter of the compound.

INT. A GOVERNMENT COMPOUND - DAY

The place was originally an army barracks, but has been converted
for civilian use. It is austere. Simple. George Foreman looks
around and is dissatisfied with what he sees.

GEORGE

I ain't stayin' here.

BULA

Excuse?

GEORGE

I ain't stayin' in this place.

BULA

But the training grounds are right
across the way. Nothing could be more
convenient. We have rooms for your
people...

GEORGE

(to Dick Sadler)
Come on, we going to find a hotel.

As George leaves, Ali takes the opportunity to get in his first
poke at Foreman:

ALI

I'm gonna be happy to stay here. Good place
to train. Good place to get your mind right.
George, he gonna have trouble. I'm gonna
be inside his head. I'm gonna say things to
him he don't know how to hear. He can't be
in no regular place to train. He gonna have
to hide off somewhere. Gonna try to keep
me out of his head. Ain't gonna work.

DREW "BUNDINI" BROWN, the self-appointed jester of Ali's men
picks up the riff.

BUNDINI

Gonna float like a butterfly, sting like a
bee. Gonna knock out that big ol' George
Foreman in less than three. 'Cause he's a...

ALI AND BUNDINI
(in unison)
B-a-a-a-d, b-a-a-a-d man.

Foreman makes a dismissive gesture, waving away Ali's remarks. But the very fact that he has even acknowledged them lets us know that Ali is already starting to get to him.

INT. THE LOBBY OF THE INTERCONTINENTAL HOTEL - DAY

This is the fanciest hotel in Zaire. Foreman and his entourage make their way across the lobby. GOVERNMENT OFFICIALS carry their luggage. Bula walks with Foreman, trying to be of help.

BULA

If I might suggest...
 (nodding toward Foreman's dog)
When the Belgians ran Zaire, it was then
the Belgian Congo, they used dogs like
these on our people. Now they are hated.
Maybe it would be best...

GEORGE

The dog's name is Daggo. And he stays
with me.

BULA

It's just.

GEORGE

He's stayin'.

INT. THE TRAINING CENTER - DAY

A boxing ring has been set up for sparring. Around the area there is also a speed bag, various pieces of gym equipment, and a heavy bag. George is working the heavy bag while a TELEVISION CREW films him training. Dick Sadler holds the bag; his body jolts with every thump from George's powerful fists. George SEES Ali and his PEOPLE ENTER the training center, waiting for their turn to train. Sadler looks at his watch, says to George.

SADLER

Time, champ.

George shakes his head, turns to the Television crew.

GEORGE

See this bag. Called a heavy bag. Weighs
maybe eighty, a hundred pounds.

George begins to punch at a furious pace, each blow a sledge hammer. With each punch, Sadler's whole body is shaken. A huge dent appears in the bag. Watching George attack the heavy bag is like watching a wrecking ball demolishing a building.

GEORGE

These are the kind of punches, break a
man's ribs.
     (calling over to Ali)
That hurt, don't it Ali? Gettin' a rib
broke? Every breath gonna pain you.
     (talking to reporters again)
Kidneys. Gut. Break your spine if you
ain't strong enough.

THUD, THUD, THUD. Heavy telling blows. Frighteningly powerful. George picks up the pace a little more. Sweat pours from his body as he sets out to demolish the heavy bag and all it represents. Ali watches, knows the message George is trying to send to him: this is what he is going to do to Ali. Not one to let any opportunity for psychological advantage be passed up, Ali wades in:

ALI

You can go now, chump. I ain't gonna
hurt you.

GEORGE

Don't want to hear that.

The television crew is eating this up. Their camera swings from one fighter to the next.

ALI

George Foreman wants to keep his mind
undisturbed because he's got a lot to worry
about. He has to face *me*, and I hit back.

The two fighters stare at each other; the battle is engaged. A TV PERSON asks George a question:

TV PERSON

Does that bother you, when he says these
things?

GEORGE

He gonna have to talk now. Ain't gonna
be much time for him to say nothin' in the
ring. Pretty much, I get in a ring with a man,
down he goes. I guess I was Muhammad Ali,
I'd stay away from them big words. Might
not be time to get 'em out.

George glares over at Ali. BOOM! BOOM! BOOM! George's fists sink deep into the heavy bag. Harder and harder. Their dull

THUDS resonate in the uncarpeted room.

ALI

> You mummy.

Ali holds his arms out stiffly in front of his body, walks around awkwardly. How you gonna catch me?

ALI

> (making a mummy sound:)
> Uuuugh.

George fires one last devastating punch into the heavy bag. THWAP! As he walks way, we HOLD ON the bag. Even now, it is covered with dents from the force of Foreman's blows. Ali SEES the bag. You can tell that the wheels are turning in his mind, taking this information into account.

INT. INTERCONTINENTAL HOTEL - DAY

Bundini Brown is passing some money to a BELLBOY.

BUNDINI

> I don't want you to poison Foreman. You
> just tell him you heard people talkin'
> 'bout poisoning him. Right?

The bellboy nods that he understands. Brown presses the money into his hands.

BUNDINI

> All right! My man! You tell your friends,
> too. I got money for all of 'em.

He winks at the bellboy conspiratorially. The bellboy gives him the thumbs up sign. Both men grin.

EXT. THE ZAIRE HIGHWAY - DAY - ANGLED THROUGH THE WINDSHIELD OF A CAR

Ali, his jogging clothes still dry, chats with some Zairean PEOPLE. He play-boxes with a twelve year old BOY, much to the amusement of the BOY'S FRIENDS.

INT. THE MOVING CAR - DAY

George Foreman looks out the window at Ali playing around. He holds up his hand for the DRIVER to stop the car.

> ### GEORGE
> You better train better than that you
> want to get in the ring with me.

Ali whispers conspiratorially to the Zaireans. They nod, begin to chant at George:

> ### ZAIREANS
> Ali boma ye! Ali boma ye!

> ### GEORGE
> What the hell is that?

> ### ZAIREAN DRIVER
> It means, "Ali, kill him!"

> ### SADLER
> He can get the whole country shouting
> for him, ain't gonna help him one lick
> once he gets in that ring.

George nods his affirmation, but even so, the scene bothers him. He motions for the driver to go on. "Ali, boma ye!" follows after the car as it drives away down the highway.

INT. GEORGE'S HOTEL SUITE – DAY

A BELLBOY brings in a food tray for George's girlfriend. She is just about to tuck into a juicy steak when George comes out of the bathroom, SEES the food, SEES the bellboy.

GEORGE
Where that come from?

GIRLFRIEND
Room service. I wanted a steak.

George picks up the food tray, puts it back on the cart.

GEORGE
Get it out of here. When the bellboy doesn't move fast enough for his taste: Get it out! The bellboy takes the food away.

GIRLFRIEND
What in the world is the matter with you George Foreman?

GEORGE
I got food comin' in from Europe, from the States. I don't see it opened in front of me, I don't see that box unsealed, we ain't eatin' it, we ain't drinkin' it.

GIRLFRIEND
You're getting crazy. You're making me crazy.

GEORGE
These bastards'd poison me in a second if they got the chance. Ain't no one gonna *boma ye* me.

GIRLFRIEND

I'm hungry.

GEORGE

We'll eat when my food gets here. Now
stop botherin' me.

George walks away. His girlfriend has a mind of her own, however,
and she has had just about all she is going to take:

GIRLFRIEND

George Foreman, I have had just about
enough of you. You have been mean.
You have been nasty. You don't want to
do anything. I came here to have some
fun. But, this... This is the last straw. I
will not be talked to like that. Now you
apologize right this instant.

George waves her off dismissively, walks back into the other room.

GIRLFRIEND

Fine! I'll have someone come get my
things.

The girlfriend SLAMS out of the suite.

INT. THE TRAINING CENTER - DAY

George is working with a SPARRING PARTNER, cutting off
the ring. The sparring partner tries to run, tries to slide away, but
each time George steps in, cuts off the ring, and backs him into
the ropes. Dick Sadler watches from nearby, nods his head with
satisfaction at what he sees. A REPORTER is by ringside. George
talks to the man, even as he works out with the sparring partner.

GEORGE

Ain't no way for Ali to win this fight. See
how I cut off the ring. Gonna be bad for
Ali tomorrow.

REPORTER

You think it's going to be a good fight?

GEORGE

It's gonna be...

WE HEAR GEORGE'S ANSWER OVER THE NEXT SCENE:
EXT. THE KINSHASHA STADIUM - NIGHT

The stadium is filled with PEOPLE. The CAMERA CREWS,
PRINT JOURNALISTS, TV PERSONALITIES, and
CELEBRITIES of every kind are there, too.

GEORGE'S VOICE
(continuing from the previous scene) ...
It's gonna be a rightful fight.

Muhammad Ali dances in the ring, shaking his head and limbs,
loosening up.

INT. GEORGE'S DRESSING ROOM - NIGHT

George is ready to go, but he isn't making any moves for the
door. Let him sit out there for a while. Give him some time to get
nervous. He's not the only one who can play games.

EXT. THE KINSHASHA STADIUM - NIGHT

The CROWD is getting impatient. The reporters are buzzing
about, filling time. Everyone is on edge, but Ali, who is in his
element: the eyes of the world are upon him. He goes from one

side of the ring to the other, CALLS OUT to the crowd like a preacher at a revival urging the congregation for a response.

ALI

Ali, *boma ye!* Ali, *boma ye!*

The CROWD returns his chant with a ROAR: "ALI BOMA YE!" Ali whips the crowd into a frenzy, and as it reaches its noisy climax, George Foreman enters the arena, HEARS the CHANT in full force: "ALI, BOMA YE!"

George makes his way down the aisle to the ring. He passes by his girlfriend... sitting in the section for Ali's friends. George does not look happy at this revelation. He glares at her for a moment, then goes on.

George and Ali meet at the center of the ring to get their instructions from the REFEREE. George does his best to stare Ali down, trying to intimidate him, but he is met with:

ALI

You have heard of me since you were a
little boy. Now, you must meet me, your
master!

George and Ali stare at each other—eye to eye ... and George blinks, perhaps surprised by Ali's remarks. He recovers quickly, taps Ali's gloves with his own, letting him know that now it starts for real.

VARIOUS ANGLES - TO COVER

George stands in his corner. Ali stands in his. The bell RINGS and the fight is on. The first round begins with George stalking

Ali, trying to cut off the ring. But Ali is fast, perhaps faster than George expected was possible. Ali lets loose with a right lead, the hardest punch to land without getting hit in return, but land it he does. The crowd ROARS.

Again and again in the first round Ali dances, peppers George with lightning fast punches—with right leads. It is a furious pace and a tremendous display of athleticism and boxing skills.

Howard Cosell comments from ringside:

> COSELL
> We are witnessing a tremendous display
> of boxing skills from Muhammad Ali.
> The years seem to have melted away, but
> it can only be a matter of time before he
> tires. No one could continue at this pace.
> And when he slows …

As if in answer to Cosell, George, for the first time, catches Ali with a devastating hook. Ali pedals away, fires a few more jabs, but it is clear he felt this one. It is clear that it is only a matter of time before George tracks him down again. The bell RINGS, sounding the end of the round.

George's corner works on him, pleased with the progress of things.

> SADLER
> That's the way, baby. Track him down. Get
> him on those ropes …

In Ali's corner there is frenetic activity. ANGELO DUNDEE spits out instructions:

DUNDEE

You're doing good. You're doing good.
Stick and move. Keep moving.You got to
keep moving.

Ali is not paying attention. He is staring across the ring at Foreman, mapping out his own strategy. Ali stands before the bell rings. He looks at Foreman, calculating what to do, assessing his best tactics.

The bell SOUNDS and both fighters head for the center of the ring, and then it happens ... Ali backs into the ropes, puts up his hands in what is now the famous rope-a-dope pose, and waits for Foreman to go after him.

George charges in, punches Ali furiously. Ali covers and ducks, and takes some blows as his corner CRIES URGENTLY for him to get off of the ropes. But Ali stays.

George lays into Ali, the way he laid into the heavy bag. Ali tries to shift with the blows, dissipate their force. He talks to George, urging him on, like a Picador provoking a bull to make him attack.

ALI

Is that it? Is that all you got?

The buzzer sounds to indicate that there is thirty seconds left. Ali comes off the ropes just long enough to sting George with a flurry of blows and then George is on him again, but the bell RINGS. The round is over.

There is pandemonium over in Ali's corner.

DUNDEE

What the hell are you doing? Stay off
those ropes? Stay away from him!

ALI

I know what I'm doing.

Over in George's corner there is exuberance and excitement.

SADLER

Pound him. Pound him. Put him away.

GEORGE

I'm gonna kill him.

George, filled with hatred and rage, glares across the ring at Ali.

VARIOUS ANGLES - A MONTAGE

The ROUND GIRLS come and go. Ali backs into the ropes,
taunts George. Again and again George punches Ali, trying to
hurt him, trying to end the fight. At the end of every round,
Ali comes out with a stinging flurry that seems to catch George
unawares, stinging him and angering him, but taking the steam
out of him as well. George's punches slow. His breathing is more
and more labored. George's corner is more and more worried.
They urge him to take Ali out, to end it. Ali sits in his corner as
the ring girl walks around with the card letting people know that
round seven is over.

ALI

This is it. He's ready to go. He's mine.

DUNDEE

Well do it for Christ's sake and stop
screwing around.

ALI

I just wanted to play with him a little,
but he's done now. He's goin' down.

VARIOUS ANGLES - TO COVER

The bell rings and Ali lets himself be taken over to the ropes, but George is slow now, and tired. Ali gauges Foreman's remaining abilities, and after the first few seconds adjudges the time to be right.

Ali comes off the ropes, peppering George with a series of jabs, something George has not seen a lot of from Ali. George appears confused. He tries to swat the punches away, like they were flies biting at him. But he is too late; the punches land and are gone before he can retract his arm. And then comes the overhand right—just as George is coming in.

GEORGE'S HEAD snaps around from the force of the punch.

VARIOUS ANGLES - TO COVER (SLOW MOTION)

Ali follows with another punch and for the first time in his career, George is knocked out. His legs buckle underneath him and he begins to fall, like a corkscrew turning in a clockwise direction. His arms flay about, the whites of his eyes show, and foam flecks his mouth.

George Foreman, the giant, tumbles to the ground and cannot get up. Ali is exuberant. The crowd is beside itself. The press is astonished. No one can believe it. Utter pandemonium.

We FREEZE FRAME on the famous shot of Ali, arms raised, as George falls to the canvas in an awkward spiral. Over this image we HEAR George talking to his congregation:

GEORGE (V.O.)

I could never get over that moment.
Never. Of all the demons that haunted
me, that was the worst.

INT. GEORGE'S CHURCH - DAY

George is in his church, pacing back and forth, worked up, but enjoying the release of getting all of this out of his system.

GEORGE

After that fight … So many things.
But most of all, envy. That's a bad sin,
envy. Eats away at you. I wanted what
Muhammad Ali had. He had my title.
He had people's respect. And all I knew
was that I had this great big hole in me
that I wanted to fill. Didn't think about
the Lord. Everything I wanted or needed,
Muhammad had it. Shame and envy go
hand in hand, 'cause when someone else
got all those things you want, well ain't
nothin' you got worth a damn. It just eats
at you and eats at you.

INT. GEORGE'S HOTEL SUITE - DAY

George sits on a couch, wearing a hat and big sunglasses so that no one can see his swollen face and eyes. Dick Sadler is trying to coax George out of the room.

SADLER

George, they waitin' on you.

Sadler goes to the hotel TV, turns it to a channel which shows the press conference. The sound is off, but we can SEE Ali, and his entourage. We can SEE much of George's retinue. But no George.

                    SADLER
          You got to take off them glasses and hat.
          Stop hidin'. Talk to the press. Sooner or
          later, you're gonna have to. You don't do
          it now, it's gonna get in your head.

                    GEORGE
          Just leave me the hell alone. I ain't talkin'
          to no one.

On the TV screen, George can see his former girlfriend sitting behind Ali. He smashes the table with his fist.

                    GEORGE
          Go on. Get out of here!

A reluctant Dick Sadler goes. George watches the press conference, SEES an animated Ali talking, mugging for the press. Filled with rage, he says to no one in particular:

                    GEORGE
          I'm a goddamned millionaire now and I
          can do any goddamned thing I want.

INT. A ROLLS ROYCE SHOWROOM (HOUSTON) - DAY

Twenty tons of gleaming steel and paint occupies the showroom, one beautiful car after another. George walks past one car and then another, deciding on a color, admiring the design lines, filled with avarice, and more importantly, a need to impress. A

SALESMAN trails behind George, caught up in George's wake like the tail of kite in a big wind.

George looks at the sticker prices of the cars as he goes, stops in front of what appears to be the biggest, most garish car on the floor.

GEORGE
This the most expensive car you got?

SALESMAN
This is the pinnacle of automotive achievement. The very essence of…

GEORGE
There ain't nothin' better? You don't have one that's more expensive?

SALESMAN
You can have the grill and trim plated with real gold if you want. We can do that. But it has to be done custom.It's very expensive, all done by hand. By artisans, masters at their craft.

GEORGE
That's what I want then. The best of the best; that's me.

EXT. GEORGE'S RANCH – DAY

This is a new home for George, with land as far as the eye can see. George is feeding raw meat to a tiger as a slightly uncomfortable Dick Sadler watches in the B.G.

A PHOTOGRAPHER snaps pictures for a magazine article while George extemporizes about the glories of his life:

GEORGE

I'm buying some lions next. Gonna walk
'em with me like they was kittens. You
see these tigers? I got animals of all kinds
here. Houston Zoo delivers fresh food
for 'em to me. Forty thousand dollars a
month it cost me.

An ASSISTANT CALLS OUT from another part of the ranch.

ASSISTANT

We're ready for you now, Mr. Foreman.

George goes over to where the photo layout has been arranged.
Five men – standing just outside of camera range – are supposed
to help George hoist a bull on his shoulders, making it look like
George is holding the bull up all by himself.

Everyone gets into place, but then something goes wrong. The
pulley rope breaks and George finds himself with an unhappy,
1200 pound steer draped around his shoulders.

GEORGE

You see how strong I am? You see?

Dick Sadler shakes his head, embarrassed for George, but there is no
talking sense to him.

ANOTHER ANGLE - LATER

The photo crews are packing up their equipment, getting ready
to leave. George takes Dick Sadler aside.

GEORGE

I been thinkin', 'bout what I want to do
next. See, people got to know I still got
stamina. What they saw in Zaire, that
wasn't the real George. That was a fluke.
What I want you to do ... I'm gonna
fight five guys in one night. Three rounds
each. I'll whup 'em all. Everyone'll see.

SADLER

George, that ain't gonna prove nothin'.
Gonna be embarrassin'.

GEORGE

Just set it up. 'Cause if you can't... There's
a lot of managers just love to have George
Foreman.

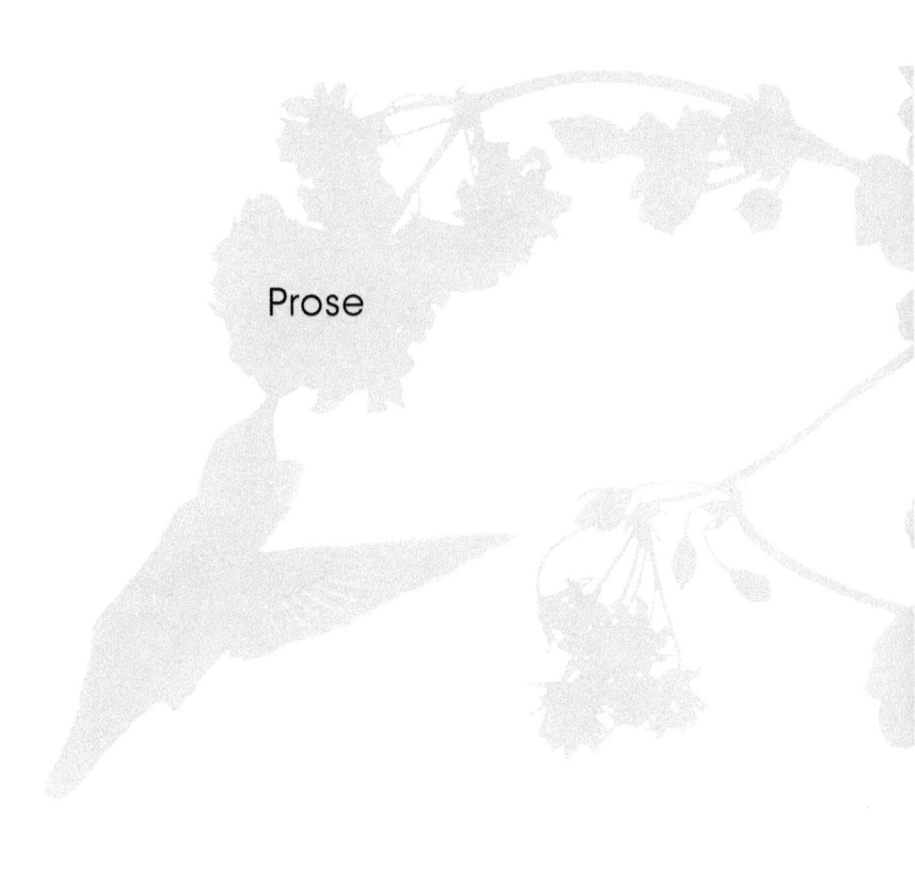

Prose

Aguas vivas y pozos secos

(Living Water and Dry Wells)

Josiah Guzik

In Santo Domingo, a small, drought stricken northern Mexico town, the fever of thirst found many water buckets aridly close to the bedrock bases of their wells. Even in the depths of the deepest well, among the cobbled, cobwebbed walls, even there the suffocating heat swirled and twisted with the crumbling algae of wetter years, so much so that even at the source where the water pooled it was tepid and warm.

The young and eager Father Jeremias captured Santo Domingo's attention, like a cactus sucks in dawn's rare and impartial dew. He and two others arrived from the Veracruz coast sharing a strong mare and a gold bound Bible. They spoke smoothly, preaching the gospel that had transformed their lives. They too had been lost — they explained — and they too had made mistakes that caused the Good God to look unfavorably upon them.

"You know, our pasts are not all that different," Father Jeremias stressed. "In fact, I come from the town of Parangaricutirimicuaro en la costa de Veracruz. Not long ago we faced a severe drought: The padre had prayed, the bishop had blessed, but the heat of the desert drew only drier and the sun, only fiercer. It wasn't until the entire town kneeled, accepting the mark of the cross and praying the sinners prayer — it wasn't until each child and every unblessed grave had been purified by the sacramental holy waters and Sunday morning Mass was full — not until these things had passed did the drought pass as well. But we had faith and, as you see, the evil one did not claim us, for I stand before you now."

The people were impressed with Father Jeremias's vibrant and moistened voice — his throat had not yet succumbed to the crackling whisper of a drought. As he went on, explaining the importance of Christ on the cross, his two helpers walked among the crowd, dolling out swigs of water from their oilskin canteens. From within the silent sweat of the crowd, Andres Diego Sebastian Álavaro de la Sierra tapped a bag of coins deep in his pocket, revealing to the friars his position in Santo Domingo, eliciting that he was perhaps the only one deserving of a second drink.

Andres Diego knew the value of a drop of water: He had, in fact, bought up nearly 80 percent of the town's wells as soon as the first heat wave licked Santo Domingo four years ago. But now, even his mouth had begun to chap around the corners and crack along the tongue.

"...And Jesus was nailed to the cross, died, and rose again on the third day, for the forgiveness of your sins," Father Jeremias continued.

Stepping onto a creaking orange crate, Andres Diego used one hand to palm his slicked-black hair, forcing his image, and placed the other over his heart, feigning endearment. "Brothers, the padre speaks wisdom. He wishes to restore life to our town, like living water to our souls."

At the urging of Andres Diego, many of the common folk followed the father's words of faith. That day, Andres Diego and 200 of the other townsfolk were baptized under the altar of living water, nibbling modestly at the body of Christ but drinking deeply from the cup of salvation.

But the flood of faith did not reach one of the driest corners of

Santo Domingo. Emiliano Colorado, his wife Esperanza Pájaro, and their three children did not hear the Fathers' words that day, for they were working the fields of Andres Diego and had not the luxury to hear of living water that afternoon. The Colorado family had the smallest parcel of land and the shallowest well of all of the inhabitants of Santo Domingo, yet they never once cringed in the heat of the drought, always watering the horses of thirsty neighbors and washing the feet of dusty travelers. Even amid the hype of the ensuing Sunday, as the rest of the town gathered for mass, Emiliano took to his family's maize, and Esperanza to a small aromatic patch of white lilies near their crumbling well.

Although nearly the entire town had kneeled, accepting the mark of the cross, and prayed the sinners prayer — although nearly every child and almost every unblessed grave had been purified by the sacramental holy waters, and Sunday mass was full — although all of these things had passed, the drought did not pass. A murmur arose from the masses after mass, suspecting that this town of Parangaricutirimicuaro, where drought had ceased was merely a story.

A week passed, the heat fevered hotly, and one third of the crops were lost. "We must have faith," Father Jeremias urged at Mass the following Sunday. "Like the prophet Elijah, who took a step of faith, pouring water on the wood that he was calling on the Lord to light. We must have faith—"

"Faith in what, Father?" interrupted a thirsty parishioner.

"Faith, compañeros, in the words of Jesus Christ. Listen to the word of the Lord," he paused and held out his hand for one of the younger friars to raise up the gold bound Bible. "The words of our Savior: 'I am the living water, whoever drinks from me shall never thirst again.'"

Stepping down now off of the pulpit, Father Jeremias smiled the smile of epiphany, and directed his step toward the other friar who was holding the oilskin canteen. He lifted the canteen over his head — not unlike Abraham offering Isaac before the Lord — and with a borrowed shepherds knife, put the blade to the hide.

"This, compañeros, is faith: taking Jesus at his words." With those words he wounded the canteen, pouring the water onto the dirt floor in the plaza, muddying the sandals of those nearby. "We," he concluded with a hint of dryness now creeping into his voice, "shall never thirst again."

Acting faithfully, they returned to their ranches and gathered rocks from the pebbled soil, loaded them onto the backs of feeble mules and aged wooden handcarts, and shoveled them into their wells. All, after tossing the last handfuls of sand into the now drier wells, turned to the sky and waited for the heavens to cloud in response to their worship.

Emiliano and Esperanza, too, found themselves filling wells, although the waters they blocked were not their own, rather the wells of Andres Diego, who remained in the shade of the plaza to converse with the priests. But the well in El Ranchito Colorado remained faithlessly wet. Esperanza had said to Emiliano, "This is foolish to fill our well, it is the only source of life we have. And besides, I already have faith of my own. I have faith in you and me and our children, that we have the strength and endurance to work through this hard time."

The sun set and rose again, revealing a blue sky cursed by El Pueblo de Santo Domingo. The priests went door to door and called people to the plaza to pray. "Ask the Lord to bring rain to our dry land, like he brought fire to Elijah's pyre."

Emiliano and Esperanza remained in the field to toil in the dry soil. The sun set and rose once again, shining brightly on the parched parishioners kneeling desperately in the plaza. Now, on the second day with no water, the people of Santo Domingo were growing impatiently thirsty and with a ferocious sternness demanded the "living water" that Father Jeremias had promised.

That evening, pressured by the crowd, Father Jeremias withdrew to the edge of the town, promising to return with the water that he spoke of. Confused, lost, and desperate, he slumped down on a rock, recalling the story of Moses who drew water from a stone. The story only served to frustrate the young father who dryly tapped the stone with his walking stick. Overwhelmed, he sat down putting his head in his hands, trying to cry; but even his tears would not wet his cheeks.

In the distance a figure approached, leading a sickly sheep and a withered ox. Nearing the father, Emiliano stated his observation, "You wail and choke like you are crying, but your face is still dry." Realizing the problem, he offered the father a swallow from his half-filled canteen. The father hung his arms around Emiliano and begged him to fill the canteens of his thirsty followers. Moved by Father Jeremias' plea, Emiliano led the priest to a crumbling stone well, swirling with dust and dancing heat waves against the purpled twilight. Emiliano lowered his bucket and filled the canteens Father Jeremias had slung over his shoulder.

The next day, as the town once again clamored for water, Father Jeremias once again approached the ranchito on the outskirts of town. Emiliano met him at the well.

"My children are now thirsty, and our well level is now low because you called your people to faith. But because Esperanza and I have faith in one another, as well as in the rest of humanity, we will allow you to continue to draw from our well."

The Father, thanking Emiliano, qualified himself by explaining that the act of faith would give shortly into a long and deserved rainy season. The next day the Father was back again, this time with Andres Diego, who carted a large bucket for his household. They left with their buckets full. The next day when the Father and Andres Diego returned to the well, Emiliano was sitting on the crumbling stone wall of the well, waiting for them. He spoke: "This morning my youngest son died of heatstroke, do you still wish to take the water from my family?"

Andres Diego responded, "If we do not take this water, then our children will also grow weak and die. Do you want to be responsible for the ills of Santo Domingo?"

Emiliano, conceded to let them use the well once again.

The next day, Emiliano was once again sitting on the cobbled wall bordering the well, waiting, when Father Jeremias, Andres Diego, and now the other two friars, approached.

"Last night my daughter suffocated in dehydration. Do you still wish to take the water from my family?"

Andres Diego once again responded: "If we do not take this water, then our children will also grow weak and die. Do you want to be responsible for the ills of Santo Domingo?"

Emiliano, once again conceded sadly, adding, "It is only because of our faith in the community, our faith in all of humanity that we continue to let you draw from our well."

The next day, Emiliano was sadly tending the white lilies near the well. This time the entire town came searching for the living waters of Rancho Colorado.

"Last night my wife and my eldest son were strangled by the unforgiving heat. If you once again take this water I will no longer be here waiting for you tomorrow. Do you still wish to take this water?"

Once again, Andres Diego spoke for the town, "Emiliano, you do not wish the same fate as your family on the rest of Santo Domingo, do you? We too need this water to survive."

Emiliano nodded, accepting his neighbors' persistence he concluded, "I will fill your buckets, and I will fill your canteens, but you must know that it was not the church that sacrificed for you, but a family like your own. Salvation isn't always bound in gold pages or carried on a cross perhaps it can sometimes be found in the goodness of humanity." And Emiliano filled their buckets.

The next day, the town returned for more, but no one was there to draw water from the well. Realizing what they had done—that their cross had not brought salvation, but death—Father Jeremias and the other fathers retreated into the desert with their strong mare and gold bound book, where Father Jeremias vowed never to drink again.

Looking up into the sky, noticing the wisps of gray clouds closing-in over the town, Andres Diego opined: "Look Santo Domingo, rain; it was not the Fathers that saved us, for they have left, nor the Colorado family, for they are gone — we have saved ourselves."

That night, the clouds thundered and the rain came down in sheets, cascading into the depths of the cobbled, cobwebbed wells, and filling the streets of Santo Domingo. By morning, the only sign of life in the flood plain four miles-wide, was a small sweet scented patch of white lilies marking Santo Domingo, where once stood a small town.

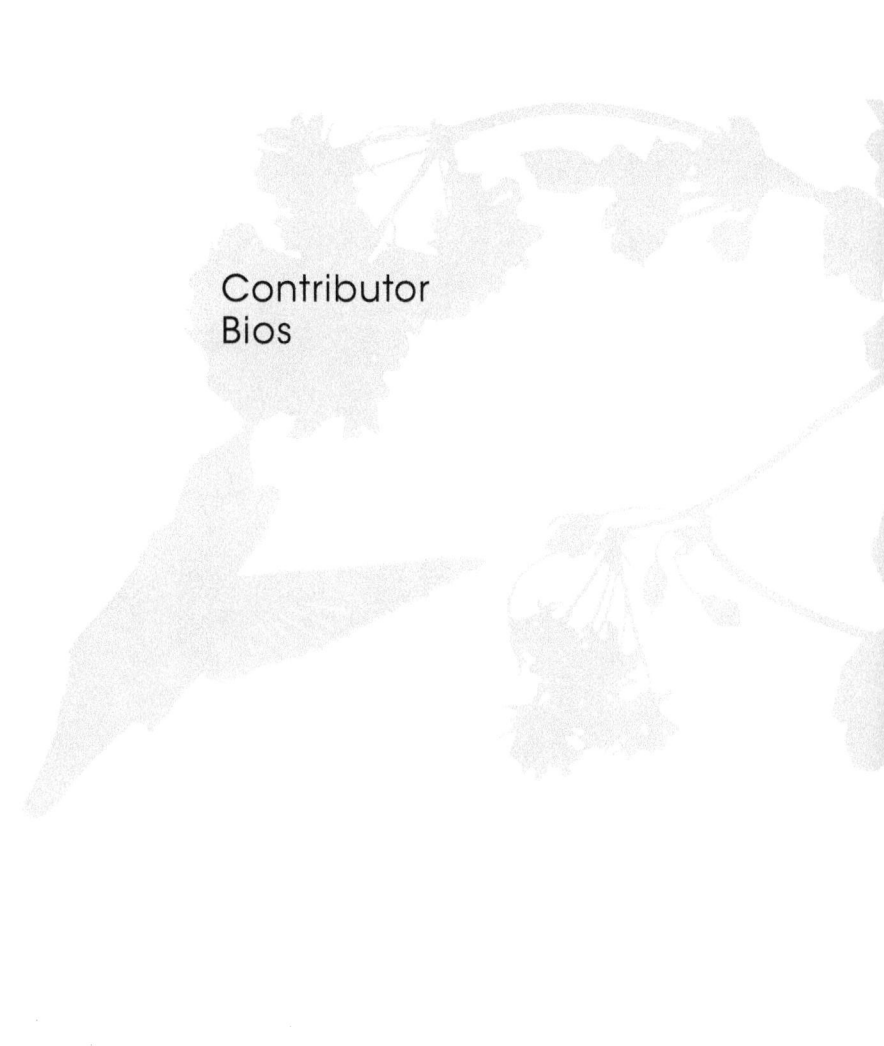

Contributor
Bios

CONTRIBUTOR BIOS

BATSIRAI E. CHIGAMA Zimbabwean-born, she is a performance poet and short story writer. She has traveled extensively in Southern Africa performing at festivals, and her poetry has appeared in 5 poetry anthologies to date. You can visit her website: www.batsiraichigama.maumbile.com and link to a resource list of poets from many African countries.

MAY K. COBB is a freelance writer based in Austin, Texas. She has spent the past several years researching and writing a book about the late jazz great, Rahsaan Roland Kirk. Her writing has appeared in *Austin Monthly Magazine* and the online edition of *JazzTimes*.

T J DEMA is a Botswanan-based international poet, and chairperson of the Writers Association of Botswana. Visit her blog and hear her read poems, along with five other poets from Botswana. She has performed in the United Kingdom, Denmark, India, France, South Africa and Zimbabwe. www.tjdema. blogspot.com

JOHN GARDINER has published 10 collections of poetry and has also been published in numerous anthologies, journals and magazines, including two *Anthologies of CA Poets* (Tebot Bach), *Spillway, Blue Satellite, Speakeasy, Write Bloody, Moon Tide Press, Poetry Flash* (Berkeley), *Windflower Press and The Comstock Journal*. In addition to hundreds of featured readings in the U.S., Gardiner has read in Russia, the Czech Republic, Italy, Germany, Ireland, and Brazil. He is a professional actor in a touring rock 'n roll Shakespeare show called "Shakespeare's Fool." Gardiner teaches Shakespeare and poetry for the Gifted Students Academy at U.C.I.

JOSIAH GUZIK is a Spanish teacher in Camden, NJ. He is an alumnus of Point Loma Nazarene University, where he studied Spanish. For two summers he worked as a field laborer, picking strawberries and weeding bell peppers alongside immigrants in the Oxnard Plain. Josiah expressed a love for writing since middle school, but did not start writing fiction until college, when a small group of friends started a monthly story telling event.

THEA IBERALL is a poet and scientist. Thea has had over 40 poems published in anthologies and journals, including *Rattle, Spillway,* and *The Southern California Anthology.* She has a poem in *Blood to Remember: American Poets on the Holocaust.* Her collection of contextual poems, *The Sanctuary of Artemis,* was published by Tebot Bach (2011).

CHERYL MERRILL Her essays have been published in *Fourth Genre, Pilgrimage, Brevity, Seems, South Loop Review, Ghoti, Alaska Quarterly Review, Adventum and Isotope.* "Singing Like Yma Sumac" was selected for the *Best of Brevity 2005* and *Creative Nonfiction #27.* It was also included in the anthology *Short Takes: Model Essays for Composition, 10th Edition.* Another essay, "Trunk," was chosen for Special Mention in *Pushcart 2008.* She is currently working on a book about elephants: *Larger than Life: Living in the Shadows of Elephants.*

JACKIE LOPEZ is founding member of the Taco Shop Poets. Her activist work slowly evolved into mysticism. She claims she had a spiritual awakening in December of 1999 and that changed her works completely. She claims she is a shaman and now writes with God. She is currently working on her novel, "Samba

Bodhisattva," in which she explains her evolution through prose. You may reach her at: peacemarisolbeautiful@yahoo.com

JOHN PERRY was born in Alaska, grew up in small towns across the US, finally settling in California. He moved to Orange County in 2006 and is relatively new to the Orange County poetry scene, where he reads at several venues. He has poems published in *Interstices, An Anthology* (Wildflower Press, 2010) and the *Don't Blame the Ugly Mug Anthology*. An incurable romantic, he writes of love and loss and beaches. He is currently working on a collection of his poetry entitled *Notes on Napkins*.

ADAM RODMAN has been writing professionally since he was a sophomore in college. Both his father and his brother are writers and there are more than a few people who suspect that there is not a lick of common sense to be found in the male side of the Rodman gene pool. Adam is currently writing a historical drama and is trying to get up the nerve to attempt his first novel.

JOHN VICENT ROULEAU is completing a book poetry and prose with matched illustrations. Rouleau lives and writes just outside of San Francisco.

FARZANA VERSEY is an Indian writer based in Mumbai. She is currently a regular op-ed contributor to *The Asian Age* and *Deccan Chronicle* newspapers. Her first book, *A Journey Interrupted—Being Indian in Pakistan* was published by Harper-Collins.

BRIAN WILKES is an author, educator, Cherokee language instructor, and Native American Church leader. He lives in Marion, Kentucky.

www.ingramcontent.com/pod-product-compliance
Lightning Source LLC
Chambersburg PA
CBHW020325130626
46549CB00003B/1026

9780985558307